BETWEEN EAST AND WEST

Richard Nelson

D0839629

BROADWAY PLAY PUBLISHING INC.

357 W 20th St., NY NY 10011
212 627-1055

First printing: December 1989
ISBN: 0-88145-077-4

Book design: Marie Donovan
Word processing: WordMarc Composer Plus
Typographic controls: Xerox Ventura Publisher, Professional Extension
Typeface: Palatino
Printed on acid-free paper and bound in the USA.

ABOUT THE AUTHOR

Richard Nelson's other plays include SOME
AMERICANS ABROAD, PRINCIPIA SCRIPTORIAE
(*Broadway Play Publishing, 1986*), AN AMERICAN
COMEDY, THE RETURN OF PINOCCHIO, RIP VAN
WINKLE or THE WORKS (*Broadway Play Publishing,
1986*), BAL (*published in the Broadway Play Publishing
anthology,* ANTI-NATURALISM, *1989*), THE VIENNA
NOTES, CONJURING AN EVENT, JUNGLE COUP
(*published in the Broadway Play Publishing anthology,*
PLAYS FROM PLAYWRIGHTS HORIZONS, *1987*), and
THE KILLING OF YABLONSKI.

Richard Nelson's plays have been presented by such
theaters as The Royal Shakespeare Company in
England, The Manhattan Theatre Club, Playwrights
Horizons, The Second Stage, and The American Place in
New York, the Goodman in Chicago, and The Empty
Space in Seattle, as well as in numerous other theaters
around the country and in Europe. He has translated
and adapted Moliere's DON JUAN (*Broadway Play
Publishing, 1989*), Beaumarchais's THE MARRIAGE OF
FIGARO, Chekhov's THREE SISTERS, Brecht's
JUNGLE OF CITIES and THE WEDDING, Erdman's
THE SUICIDE, and Fo's ACCIDENTAL DEATH OF
AN ANARCHIST. He also is the author of the book for
the Broadway musical CHESS.

Nelson has received a London TIME OUT Theatre
Award, two Obie Awards, a Giles Cooper Award, a
Guggenheim Fellowship, two Rockefeller Playwriting

Grants, and two National Endowment for the Arts playwriting fellowships, the most recent being one of the NEA's first two-year grants.

For Ms. Ridder
and Her Husband

BETWEEN EAST AND WEST was first performed on
14 January 1985 at The Yale Repertory Theatre, New
Haven (Lloyd Richards, Artistic Director), with the
following cast and creative contributors:

GREGOR HASEK .... Thomas Hill
ERNA HASEK .... Jo Henderson

Director .... John Madden
Set designer .... Basha Zmyslowska
Costume designer ....Rusty Smith
Lighting designer ....David Alan Stach
Sound designer .... James Brewcsynski
Stage manager .... Margaret Adair

BETWEEN EAST AND WEST was subsequently
presented on 10 December 1987 at The Hampstead
Theatre Club, London, with the following cast:

GREGOR HASEK . . . . John Woodvine
ERNA HASEK . . . . Sheila Allen

Director . . . . David Jones
Set designer . . . . Eileen Diss
Costume designer . . . . Sue Plummer
Lighting designer . . . . Mick Hughes
Sound designer . . . . Colin Brown
Dialect coach . . . . Joan Washington
Stage managers . . . . .Catherine Bailey, Caroline Beale,
Nick Frankfort, and Hedda Moore

THE CHARACTERS

GREGOR and ERNA HASEK, Czech emigrés in their
fifties. He is a stage and film director; she, an actress.

NOTE

When Gregor and Erna are speaking "English", they
speak with strong accents and in a somewhat
unconfident way. When they speak "Czech", they have
either very little or no accents. In the text, the "English"
lines are capitalized.

THE SETTING

A one-room apartment, sparsely furnished, on the
upper East Side, New York City.

THE TIME

1983

THE TITLES

The TITLE given each scene should be projected all the time the scene is played and should remain in view for a few moments after the scene is over.

THE SCENES

One: THE CULMINATION
Two: EIGHT MONTHS EARLIER
Three: THE CONTEXT
Four: BEFORE
Five: AND AFTER
Six: DUSTIN HOFFMAN
Seven: THE LAND OF OPPORTUNITY
Eight: BY THE BOOTSTRAPS
Nine: SHADOWS
Ten: THE FREE WORLD
Eleven: GOING PLACES
Twelve: SIBERIA
Thirteen: HIS MEMORY
Fourteen: HER MEMORY
Fifteen: SIBERIA CONTINUED
Sixteen: A FEW DAYS BEFORE
Seventeen: ERNA RECALLS AN EARLIER SCENE
Eighteen: THE CULMINATION ENDS
Nineteen: BETWEEN EAST AND WEST

Scene One

Title: THE CULMINATION

(ERNA *sits watching television. She smokes.*)

TELEVISION: "Shouting over the cat-calls of back benchers, Mrs. Thatcher today restated her support for the deployment of American Pershing missiles on British soil. While she spoke to Parliament, an estimated crowd of 100,000 Britons staged what is being described as the largest political demonstration since the war...."

(*The door to the hallway opens and* GREGOR *enters. He wears a winter hat and coat.* ERNA *turns to him.*)

TELEVISION: "Mrs. Thatcher never referred to the Grenada invasion which has greatly strained relations with the Reagan White House. Instead she...."

(ERNA *has gotten up and turns off the television. Pause.*)

GREGOR: Do you want to tell me what you meant last night on the phone?

(*She doesn't respond. He takes off his hat and coat.*)

ERNA: You didn't have to come, Gregor.

GREGOR: I came.

ERNA: What about rehearsals?

GREGOR: They changed the schedule. We'll rehearse tonight. (*Pause*) I have to catch the next train back.

ERNA: When is the next train back?

GREGOR: One hour.

ERNA: You came back for one hour? How much does the train cost?

GREGOR: Erna, I came. *(Pause)* Erna, last night —.

ERNA: I'll bet your American actors love you. Actors always love you. I loved you.

GREGOR: Erna, last night you scared me.

ERNA: I'm scared myself.

GREGOR: What about? *(No response)* I will be back in two weeks.

ERNA: You won't come back.

GREGOR: That's a stupid thing to say and you know it.

ERNA: I know it's stupid. Yes.

(Short pause)

GREGOR: You don't have the heat on in here, do you? I'll get you a sweater.

(He moves to the closet.)

ERNA: You can't just let things slip away, Gregor.

GREGOR: What's slipping away?

(He gets the sweater.)

ERNA: Gregor....

(He stops.)

ERNA: They will take and they won't stop. The moment you give, they take. That's how it is in a country like this.

GREGOR: What do you have against this country anyway?

ERNA: I don't have anything against it. And I don't have anything for it. That's only the way you think, not me. But you won't understand that.

(Pause)

GREGOR: You've been alone too long.

ERNA: Just three weeks.

GREGOR: Why don't you come to Hartford with me.

ERNA: And sit in a hotel room? I'm sitting in this room.

GREGOR: You can watch rehearsals. You'll be treated very well. They'll adore you.

ERNA: Like they adore you.

GREGOR: Erna — what I'm doing is a job! Try to understand that — it's nothing more!

ERNA: I don't want to see you give up.

GREGOR: What have I given up?! What the hell do I have to give up?!!!

ERNA: You don't know.

GREGOR: Erna — would you like to talk to a doctor?

ERNA: A doctor? Oh that's right. In the West that's what you do, isn't it? Talk to a doctor. *(Pause)* I'd better pack.

GREGOR: You'll come to Hartford? *(Pause)* When?

ERNA: I'd better pack.

GREGOR: Come tomorrow. There's a train at ten. I'll make sure someone meets you. I'll talk to the stage manager. Erna....

(She has turned away.)

GREGOR: It'll make us both feel better, I'm sure of it.

(He puts his coat on, goes to kiss her — she doesn't respond.)

ERNA: I'm glad — you're sure of it.

GREGOR: *(At the door)* We'll go out to eat. What kind of food would you like? There's a very good Japanese restaurant near the theater....

ERNA: Japanese? Yes. That would make sense for two Czechs in America.

(He goes. She turns the television back on.)

TELEVISION: "The opposition Social Democratic Party, ignoring an appeal by former Chancellor Helmut Schmidt, said today that it could not accept the deployment of American medium-range missiles in West Germany. The decision, taken at a special party congress in Cologne, was the culmination of...."

Scene Two

Title: EIGHT MONTHS EARLIER

(The apartment eight months earlier. The day after GREGOR and ERNA's arrival in America. The apartment has a few less things; also, there is no television. GREGOR has just entered and is taking off his jacket. ERNA fusses in the kitchen.)

GREGOR: It's not at all what I expected. I expected it to be different of course, but not this different.

ERNA: How different?

GREGOR: How different did I expect it? Or how different is it?

ERNA: Whichever makes you happy, Gregor.

GREGOR: You're really not interested, are you? You know, I can't understand that, Erna.

ERNA: Who said I'm not interested?

GREGOR: It's obvious.

ERNA: Gregor, I'm interested.

GREGOR: No you're not.

ERNA: I'm listening aren't I? You were saying New York is so different.

(Pause)

GREGOR: It's nothing like Prague, Erna.

ERNA: There's only one Prague.

GREGOR: You really should have come with me. It's hard to put into words. The second I walked out onto the sidewalk I could feel it. You want to know where I went?

ERNA: Where did you go, Gregor?

GREGOR: I went into the subway. I bought a token — they don't have tickets — tokens. And I waited for a train — you can travel as far as you want on one token.

ERNA: Really?

GREGOR: And a train pulled in. In fact, two. One going in each direction.

ERNA: Did you know where you were going?

GREGOR: No. I didn't understand the map.

ERNA: But you got on the train?

GREGOR: I wanted to, Erna. I wanted to go to the end of the line. To get out where the blacks live. I wanted to see that. You don't see that in Prague.

ERNA: You don't see what?

GREGOR: A whole section of blacks. You see pictures. We've seen pictures, Erna.

ERNA: What pictures?

GREGOR: Of black sections in New York City! *(Beat)* Well, I've seen these pictures.

ERNA: So have I, Gregor.

GREGOR: So then I wanted to see for myself what it was like.

ERNA: And what was it like?

GREGOR: Erna, I do not think that is a strange thing to want to see on your first day in New York.

ERNA: Strange? Why would it be strange? It's what I would want to do. We've heard so much about those places. *(Beat)* We've seen pictures.

GREGOR: That's true.

ERNA: So what was it like?

GREGOR: The black sections?

ERNA: Yes.

GREGOR: I never got there. I never actually got on the train.

ERNA: You never got on the train?

GREGOR: No. I wanted to. But I didn't. I let the train leave. I stayed on the platform.

ERNA: I see.

GREGOR: I didn't know where they were going.

ERNA: Oh.

GREGOR: I tried to ask a black man who was standing on the platform, but my English I guess is not so good as I thought.

ERNA: Your English is very good, Gregor. My English isn't very good.

GREGOR: In any case, he didn't seem to understand.

ERNA: I see, so you stayed on the platform all this time?

GREGOR: No. I went back onto the street and walked up Fifth Avenue. And I bought some cigarettes.

(He takes out two packs.)

ERNA: Kents? You bought Kents?

GREGOR: For one dollar each.

ERNA: Each cigarette?

GREGOR: Each of these packages, Erna. For one dollar each.

ERNA: Only one dollar for American cigarettes. For Kents?

GREGOR: This is America, Erna....I bought the cigarettes and I bought an umbrella.

(He shows her a black umbrella.)

ERNA: It was raining? From up here it didn't look like it was raining.

GREGOR: I bought it from a boy on the street. I could have also bought a watch. But I just bought the umbrella. See here — it has a button. *(Presses the button and the umbrella opens)* And I went into the Plaza Hotel carrying the umbrella.

ERNA: You just walked in? Gregor, are you sure you can do that?

GREGOR: The doorman opened the door for me so I went in.

ERNA: What did you do in the hotel?

GREGOR: I went out again. Though I went out before he could open the door for me. He was busy opening the car door for a millionaire.

ERNA: For who?

GREGOR: A millionaire.

ERNA: How did you find out this man was a millionaire?

GREGOR: If you'd seen him, you'd know. I told you you should have come with me.

ERNA: I know. I will.

GREGOR: And Erna, across the street is the park and at the corner of this park were bums. Don't ask me how I knew they were bums, it was obvious. One had a plastic bag over his foot.

ERNA: Really?

GREGOR: So here was this millionaire and here was this bum. Both right there together. I guess that's democracy.

ERNA: A bum and a millionaire are democracy?

GREGOR: You know what I mean. I wanted to talk to the bum so I went up to him.

ERNA: What did you say?

GREGOR: Nothing. I never actually talked to him.

ERNA: Maybe the next time.

GREGOR: Yes.

ERNA: When you're more comfortable with English.

GREGOR: Yes. Then we can ask anybody anything.

ERNA: Not anything, Gregor.

GREGOR: What can't we ask, Erna?

ERNA: I don't know yet.

GREGOR: Then we can ask anybody anything.

ERNA: I guess so. But still be careful.

GREGOR: I'm always careful.

ERNA: That's not true.

GREGOR: Erna, can't we go one day without bringing that up, please?

(Pause)

ERNA: So what did you do after you didn't speak to the bum?

GREGOR: What would you have done?

ERNA: What *would* I have done? I think I would have bought another package of Kents.

(He takes out another pack of Kents. They look at each other and break out laughing.)

ERNA: *(Through the laughter)* Next time — I'll go too.

Scene Three

Title: THE CONTEXT

(ERNA alone at the table, reading New York Times. *To her side are three dictionaries — a Czech/English-English/Czech; a Czech; and an English. She refers to these often. She smokes and drinks coffee as she reads. Even though it is morning, she has been up for quite awhile and is dressed.)*

ERNA: *(In a loud voice, reading)* "IS REAGAN'S FOREIGN POLICY OVERHEATED OR WARMING UP?"

(She pronounces 'Reagan' as 'Regan.')

What is this 'OVERHEATED OR WARMING UP?' Is it like a joke?

GREGOR: *(Off, from the bathroom)* Is what like a joke?

ERNA: "IS REAGAN'S FOREIGN POLICY OVERHEATED OR WARMING UP?" I don't understand.

GREGOR: *(Entering from the bathroom, unshaven and in his bathrobe)* It's Reagan, not Regan. Regan's some other important official. The exchequer, I think. *(He goes to the stove, takes a coffee mug.)* What don't you understand?

ERNA: The joke. "OVERHEATED OR WARMING UP".

GREGOR: *(Putting hot water into his mug)* Why is that a joke?

(He goes to the refrigerator.)

ERNA: That's what I'm asking. Is it a joke — a play on words?

GREGOR: *(With his head in the refrigerator)* I wouldn't call American foreign policy just a play on words, Erna.

(He takes an egg out of the refrigerator.)

ERNA: The headline, not the policy. I'll look it up myself.

(She begins to go through the dictionary. He starts to cook his egg.)

GREGOR: Josef was telling me last night that outside of New York City nearly everyone thinks like Ronald Reagan.

ERNA: *(Going through the dictionary)* Did he say why?

GREGOR: He said that in New York City they don't think like him at all. Because here everyone's a Democrat.

ERNA: Oh. *(Pause)* Is Josef a Democrat?

GREGOR: I didn't want to ask.

ERNA: Why didn't you want to ask?

GREGOR: I didn't know if I should, Erna. Outside of New York City are the farms. Though there are the steel mills in the west, too.

ERNA: Certainly the steelworkers are Democrats, Gregor.

GREGOR: Steelworkers are usually socialists, Erna. *(Pause)* It's like a car.

ERNA: What is?

GREGOR: "OVERHEATED OR WARMING UP."

ERNA: Like a car?? Oh. I see.

(She puts away the dictionary.)

GREGOR: When a car runs too long it gets overheated, but when you start it up....

ERNA: I said — I understand now, Gregor.

(He shrugs. His egg has boiled, he starts to take it out.)

ERNA: *(Without looking up)* That egg in the refrigerator is bad.

(He looks at the egg.)

GREGOR: Then why was it in the refrigerator?

ERNA: *(Looking at the paper)* I was waiting for you to go shopping with me.

GREGOR: Why do you need me to take you shopping? And that doesn't explain the egg.

ERNA: I don't need you to take me shopping.

GREGOR: If you don't need me to take you, why don't you go by yourself?

ERNA: I have. *(Short pause)* Twice.

GREGOR: So why was the bad egg in the refrigerator?

ERNA: Can't you just throw it away? *(She sets down her paper.)* I'll throw it away.

GREGOR: I can throw the egg away. *(He does.)* There, I've done it.

ERNA: How sweet of you.

(Pause)

GREGOR: *(Looking into the refrigerator)* Is the cheese bad too?

(She shrugs without looking up.)

GREGOR: It's bad.

ERNA: There's bread. It's hard, but you can toast it. *(She gets up.)* Here. I'll toast it for you.

GREGOR: I can toast it.

(He takes out the bread, takes a large knife out of a drawer.)

ERNA: It's already sliced. It comes that way.

GREGOR: I can see that.

ERNA: Then why the knife?

GREGOR: *(Putting down the knife)* Habit.

(Pause)

ERNA: *(Reads)* "MR. REAGAN TRIED TO RUN OVER THE OPPOSITION WITH A HARD-LINE APPROACH." What is this 'RUN OVER'?

GREGOR: *(Trying to mime it)* You know — RUN OVER.

ERNA: Oh. Like with a car again.

GREGOR: Yes.

ERNA: Americans do love their cars, don't they? Least that's what everyone always says.

GREGOR: Who's everyone, Erna?

ERNA: Don't tell me you never heard that before?

GREGOR: Of course I've heard that.

ERNA: Then the person you heard it from is one of the everyone who's always saying it.

GREGOR: But they don't say it here.

ERNA: Everyone doesn't live here, Gregor. Or have you already forgotten that?

GREGOR: I haven't forgotten anything.

ERNA: *(She turns to stare at him.)* No? *(Pause. She turns back.)* Good. *(Pause)* You should read the paper too, Gregor, and find out what's happening in the world.

GREGOR: You mean at home? I don't need a newspaper to tell me what's happening at home.

ERNA: Oh, you're only interested in what's happening at home? Isn't what's happening here important to you too? I thought you were the one who had to live here.

GREGOR: I read the paper, damnit.

ERNA: You read a theater paper. That's not a paper.

GREGOR: I read what I need to read. We need to know certain things.

ERNA: What do we need to know that's in a theater paper?

GREGOR: Who's important — for instance.

ERNA: Oh. So who's important?

GREGOR: A million people.

ERNA: A million people can't be important — even here.

GREGOR: *(Throws up his hands)* For example — Dustin Hoffman's important!

ERNA: Is that what you've learned, that Dustin Hoffman's important? We could have stayed home to find that out.

GREGOR: *(Moves to the bathroom)* Besides, Erna, why should I bother to read the newspaper when you always read it to me?

ERNA: I don't read it to you — I ask you questions.

GREGOR: If I don't know what's happening — why ask me questions?

ERNA: Good question. Though I think that has something to do with what choices I have.

GREGOR: There are plenty of people who you could talk to.

ERNA: But they don't want to talk to me, Gregor.

GREGOR: Keep telling yourself that and it'll turn out being true.

ERNA: Come shopping with me and you'll find out it already is.

GREGOR: I see — now we are back to the subject of my taking you shopping.

ERNA: I didn't know we ever left it. I've just been waiting for you to finish breakfast.

GREGOR: I've finished! There's no food.

ERNA: That's my point about the shopping.

GREGOR: Fine. You want me to take you shopping. I'll take you shopping! Get your purse!

ERNA: Now? You aren't dressed!

GREGOR: *(He goes to the bathroom door.)* Damnit, I'll get dressed! We'll go shopping. We'll come back to this apartment. We'll lock the door. You can continue reading me the newspaper.

ERNA: I don't read you the newspaper.

GREGOR: *(Goes in and then comes out)* What the hell, maybe I won't even shave today. After listening to you, you have to ask yourself, what is the goddamn point!

(GREGOR closes the door. Pause. Telephone rings.)

ERNA: Telephone, Gregor.

GREGOR: *(Off)* Get it.

ERNA: Gregor!

GREGOR: Erna, pick up the phone!

(She lets it ring.)

GREGOR: Erna! *(He hurries out of the bathroom with shaving cream on his face. Into the phone:)* HELLO? OH,

YES. THAT IS VERY NICE. BUT... YES, BUT I DO NOT THINK SO. VERY BUSY TONIGHT. SO THANK YOU. YES, I HUG YOU. GOODBYE. *(He hangs up.)*

ERNA: I thought you weren't going to shave.

GREGOR: That was Josef.

ERNA: *(Shrugs)* He doesn't want to talk to me. *(She takes a cigarette.)*

GREGOR: What makes you think that?

ERNA: I don't think I'm American enough for him.

GREGOR: And I am?

ERNA: You've been trying hard enough, Gregor. *(Pause)* What did he want?

GREGOR: He invited us to watch the fireworks tonight on the Hudson River.

ERNA: Tonight?

GREGOR: It's American Independence Day.

ERNA: Today?

(She opens her paper.)

GREGOR: That's yesterday's paper. You won't find out anything in there.

ERNA: No. I bought it this morning.

GREGOR: This morning?

ERNA: Yes.

GREGOR: You can go out and buy the paper, but you can't buy food?

ERNA: You can't buy food from a machine, Gregor.

(He moves back toward the bathroom.)

ERNA: You told Josef no?

GREGOR: Of course I told him no.

ERNA: You didn't ask me if I wanted to go.

GREGOR: Because I knew you wouldn't want to go.

ERNA: Who will be there?

(GREGOR *shrugs.*)

ERNA: I couldn't go.

GREGOR: I didn't ask you to go, Erna.

ERNA: That's just what I was saying.

GREGOR: You want me to call him back and see if we can still go and then I can ask you and you can tell me you don't want to go so I can tell him again we can't go?

(*Pause*)

(*She looks away. He goes back into the bathroom, then suddenly comes out.*)

GREGOR: Just what is it that you want, Erna?!!!

(*Pause. He stares at her. She gets up, gets another cigarette, lights it, and goes by him into the bathroom, closing the door. GREGOR takes his toast and butters it. He takes it to the table and sits down to eat, still with shaving cream on his face. ERNA comes out of the bathroom — her eyes red from crying. She still smokes. They look at each other.*)

ERNA: You don't have any meetings today?

GREGOR: It's a holiday.

(*She nods.*)

GREGOR: So I can take you shopping.

(*She nods, and again takes the newspaper. Pause.*)

ERNA: (*Reading:*) "THAT IS A LONG HAUL WITH UNCERTAIN RESULTS." Gregor, what does this 'LONG HAUL' mean?

GREGOR: 'LONG HAUL?' I don't know. Read me the whole sentence, maybe I can figure it out from the context.

Scene Four

Title: BEFORE

(Early evening. ERNA *and* GREGOR *sit on the couch — waiting, dressed to go out.)*

ERNA: What time is it now?

(He shows her his watch.)

ERNA: Is he late? I haven't learned what's late here.

*(*GREGOR *shrugs. Pause.)*

ERNA: Are you worried about showing the film?

GREGOR: No. *(Pause)* Just remembering what I went through to make it. That's all. They wouldn't understand here.

ERNA: Other people made it too, Gregor. *(Short pause)* I made it too. Or don't you remember?

GREGOR: You acted in it.

ERNA: Ah.

GREGOR: You were wonderful, Erna. It'll be nice to see you acting again.

ERNA: Who says I've ever stopped acting?

*(*GREGOR *laughs to himself and nods. Pause.)*

GREGOR: There were things I went through to make this film that even you never imagined.

ERNA: Like what?

GREGOR: Never mind. It's best to forget about all that now.

ERNA: Like what? You mean with the authorities? You think you were the only person to have problems with the authorities? Everyone had problems with the authorities.

GREGOR: Not everyone, Erna. Or have you already forgotten how they do things at home?

ERNA: Who didn't have problems with the authorities, Gregor?

GREGOR: Klima for instance. He never had a problem.

ERNA: Klima's in prison now, Gregor.

GREGOR: I don't mean now, I mean then. When we were all making films. They always approved Klima's scripts. With the rest of us, it was maybe one out of three, but with Klima.... And that's just how it was with my film, within a week of submitting it, Klima's script was approved. Just like that. Who knew why?

ERNA: So just like that they approved Klima's script —.

GREGOR: They always did, Erna.

ERNA: Then what was the big problem?

(Short pause. He smiles, turns to her, and whispers.)

GREGOR: *(Whispering)* They approved *a* script, Erna, but that's not to say they approved *the* script.

ERNA: You mean there were two scripts for your film?

GREGOR: No, there was only Klima's script. You think I was crazy? But there was also a script in my head, one that hadn't — and maybe couldn't — be written down.

ERNA: I didn't know that.

GREGOR: No one knew about it — except the cameraman; his family too had been on the list after the war so we understood each other.

ERNA: So there was a big difference between Klima's and your scripts?

GREGOR: A very big difference.

ERNA: And the script I was given on the set — then that was your script.

GREGOR: No, no, that was Klima's.

ERNA: Gregor — but that's the script I learned my lines from.

GREGOR: I know that. Klima was there all the time. I couldn't exactly change his script when he was there.

ERNA: But then you shot Klima's script.

GREGOR: I shot it, yes. But I shot it *as if* it were my script. I made it very different.

ERNA: Oh.

(She laughs to herself.)

GREGOR: What's funny? It was different, Erna. It wasn't the script Klima had in mind at all.

ERNA: But they were his words.

GREGOR: You can say a lot of different things with the same words! *(Pause)* Remember the house?

ERNA: The house in the film?

GREGOR: Yes, Erna.

ERNA: Of course I remember it. The big white farm house. The whole film was shot in that house

GREGOR: I went through hell to shoot my film in that house! I could have shot Klima's script in any old farm house. But not mine. Oh they tried to make me. I spent six months looking for that house. See, I had to have a house just like the one I grew up in. Like the house I was born in. Like the house they took away from us. *(Short pause)* Nothing else would do.

(Pause)

ERNA: Gregor, I didn't know —.

GREGOR: In *my* script there had to be this house. *(Short pause)* I didn't dare just use my family's old house. *(Short pause)* That would have made them very suspicious. *(Short pause)* My house. *(He smiles to himself.)* My film. *(Pause)* See — they won't understand here.

ERNA: *(Taking his hand)* Gregor —.

(Door buzzer)

GREGOR: That's Josef now.

Scene Five

Title: AND AFTER

(Later that evening. GREGOR is getting undressed. ERNA sits.)

ERNA: We don't belong. I hope that is clear to you now.

GREGOR: Actually I was just thinking the opposite, Erna.

ERNA: Yes?

GREGOR: Yes. *(He gets his pajamas out of a drawer.)* Everyone liked the film, Erna.

ERNA: Everyone wasn't at the cinema, Gregor.

GREGOR: Everyone who was liked it, Erna.

ERNA: You talked to everyone then?

GREGOR: I talked to everyone who talked to me.

ERNA: *(Snickers to herself)* That's just what I mean.

GREGOR: Erna, they liked it. My film was liked. You can't deny that.

ERNA: And therefore you think they like you.

GREGOR: I didn't say that.

ERNA: If they like your work, they like you. That's how you think.

GREGOR: That is not how I think, Erna.

ERNA: Or is it — since they said they liked your film, then you like them.

GREGOR: All I said was — they liked it. Damnit Erna, isn't that enough for now?

ERNA: I don't know — is it?

(He ignores her and goes into the bathroom to change.)

ERNA: So maybe they liked it, but that doesn't mean they enjoyed it. I'm not sure they could ever enjoy it like it was meant to be enjoyed.

GREGOR: *(Off)* How was it meant to be enjoyed??!

(Pause)

ERNA: You know what I mean.

(Pause)

GREGOR: *(Off)* You talked to people. What did people tell you?

ERNA: I talked to no one.

GREGOR: *(Entering, in his pajamas)* I saw you talking to the manager of the cinema, Erna.

ERNA: Yes, I talked to him.

GREGOR: What did he say about the film?

ERNA: We didn't speak about your film. You think everyone was always speaking about your film? *(Pause)* We talked about other things.

GREGOR: Good.

ERNA: I asked him how much he paid his workers.

(GREGOR has gone into the kitchen and pours himself a vodka.)

GREGOR: Workers?

ERNA: Yes.

(GREGOR drinks the vodka.)

GREGOR: You asked him how much he paid his workers? What workers, Erna?

ERNA: That's what he asked. I said, the projectionist for example.

GREGOR: And what did the manager of the cinema say?

ERNA: He said the projectionist was a student.

(GREGOR washes the glass in the sink.)

GREGOR: When I was a student, I was a projectionist. Did you know that?

ERNA: We're not talking about you now, Gregor.

(He shrugs, goes to get into bed.)

ERNA: So if the projectionist is a student, then he couldn't be considered a worker. He's an intellectual.

GREGOR: The manager of the cinema said the student was an intellectual?

ERNA: No, he just said he was a student — but isn't that what he meant?

GREGOR: *(In bed now)* I think he meant that he was a student, Erna.

(Pause. She takes another cigarette.)

GREGOR: You know you get headaches when you smoke too much.

(She shrugs.)

GREGOR: Do what you want.

ERNA: That's easy to say.

(Pause. GREGOR sits up.)

GREGOR: They said they liked it. Why would they lie?

ERNA: You're fifty-six years old and you ask why do people lie?

GREGOR: I mean in this case.

ERNA: Maybe it's not that they lied, maybe it's that you didn't understand.

GREGOR: What's not to understand? I don't understand.

ERNA: Maybe they liked it only as a foreign film, Gregor.

GREGOR: But it is a foreign film. I'm foreign. I made it. It's in Czech. There were subtitles.

ERNA: That's what I mean. They liked it because it was foreign. That doesn't mean they enjoyed it, Gregor. *(Pause)* You don't know Americans, Gregor.

GREGOR: And of course you do.

ERNA: I never claimed that. I never claimed that Americans liked me.

GREGOR: They like you, Erna. Please.

ERNA: Because they like your film, they like you. And because they like you, they like me? Is that what I'm supposed to believe?

(He rolls over, ignoring her.)

ERNA: Gregor? *(Short pause)* I don't want to lose you.

(Pause. He sits up and looks at her.)

GREGOR: Really? You seem to be trying to.

Scene Six

Title: DUSTIN HOFFMAN

(ERNA stands at the kitchen counter. GREGOR sits on the floor, opening a large box.)

(Pause. GREGOR slowly pulls out styrofoam and then a smallish television set.)

GREGOR: Maybe I should have gotten a color set, what do you think? *(No response)* It's black and white.

(Pause)

ERNA: How much did it cost?

GREGOR: The color set? *(She shakes her head.)* There was a sale. We can afford it.

ERNA: Can we?

GREGOR: And Josef said I can take it off my taxes. He said, because I'll use it for business.

ERNA: A television?

GREGOR: Hand me a butter knife.

(She does.)

ERNA: What does it mean — take it off your taxes?

GREGOR: It seems, Erna, that the government will pay for part of the television.

ERNA: The American government buys its people televisions?

GREGOR: That's what Josef says.

ERNA: Does the government make the televisions?

GREGOR: Erna, this is America.

ERNA: How much did we pay and how much did the government pay?

GREGOR: The government hasn't paid anything yet — but they will.

ERNA: How much?

GREGOR: I don't know. Ask Josef. *(He screws the antenna on with the knife.)* Look in the newspaper, they say what's on in there.

ERNA: Then how do we know we can afford it, if we don't know how much we pay?

(She hands him the paper.)

ERNA: I went to the consulate today.

(Long pause)

GREGOR: A television will help you learn English.

ERNA: I said, I went —.

GREGOR: I heard you. *(Short pause)* OUR consulate?

(She nods.)

ERNA: They had the Prague papers. Skreta's opened his MACBETH.

GREGOR: I knew that.

ERNA: They say it's spectacular.

GREGOR: Who's they, Erna? The Prague papers? Everything Skreta does they say is spectacular — since he went back.

ERNA: There were photographs — it looked spectacular. *(Pause)* So you bought a television so I would learn English.

GREGOR: I bought it because I wanted it, Erna.

ERNA: You sound like an American already. *(Pause)* The attaché asked how you were.

GREGOR: He recognized you? Did they follow you? *(She turns away.)* Erna, did they follow you?!

(She turns back, shakes her head.)

GREGOR: How do you know?

ERNA: I went through Macy's department store. I don't think it's possible to follow anyone through Macy's department store.

GREGOR: Erna, please — be careful.

ERNA: I'm the one who always has been careful.

GREGOR: Stop it!

(Pause)

ERNA: Besides, they know where we live, Gregor. Don't fool yourself.

GREGOR: If they knew where we lived, they would have been harassing us by now. Where's the newspaper with the television programs?

ERNA: It's right there, Gregor.

(He picks it up.)

ERNA: The attaché said we could come back. *(She looks at him and then away.)* Skreta went back.

GREGOR: Skreta had an exit stamp in his passport, Erna. Skreta did not escape through Yugoslavia. Skreta went on an extended holiday. We left. They'll SAY anything, Erna. Don't you know that by now? We can't go back.

(Pause)

ERNA: The attaché put an exit stamp in my passport.

(She gets up and gets her passport to show him.)

GREGOR: What did you tell them, Erna?

ERNA: There was only the attaché. I only spoke to him.

GREGOR: What did you tell him, Erna?

ERNA: There wasn't anything to say. *(Short pause)*
Gregor, I didn't plan it. I was on the bus and this man
looks up at me, he offers me his seat — in Czech. Then
he tells me how much he has admired my stage work.
He'd seen almost everything, Gregor. I told him he
wasn't old enough to have seen everything. He gave me
his card — he was the attaché's driver.

GREGOR: His driver on a bus?

(Pause)

ERNA: He said he understood, Gregor. He didn't
pressure me.

GREGOR: But you went to the consulate. *(Short pause)*
Why???!

(She looks at him, takes out a cigarette, lights it, turns away.)

ERNA: You never said how much the television cost.

(Pause)

GREGOR: Eight-three dollars. Plus tax.

ERNA: Plus tax? I thought you took it off your tax.

GREGOR: That's a different tax.

*(He turns the television on. Flips a channel. ERNA moves in
front of the television.)*

GREGOR: Try a channel.

(She shakes her head. He flips to another channel.)

GREGOR: What are you smirking about?

ERNA: American television.

(She turns away.)

GREGOR: You've seen ten seconds!!

ERNA: I've heard about it.

(She goes back to the kitchen counter. Long pause.)

GREGOR: *(Finally)* Erna, I bought the goddamn television so you would learn how to talk to people!!

ERNA: I know how to talk to people. I talked to people today!!

(She puts on her sweater.)

GREGOR: Where are you going now?

ERNA: To buy a newspaper.

(She leaves. Television is on. She returns.)

ERNA: The mail came. There's a letter from Prague.

GREGOR: From your sister?

(She hurries and opens it. GREGOR has gotten up.)

ERNA: Here, you read these pages.

(He takes them. They are devouring the letter. She happens to look up at the television.)

ERNA: Gregor?

GREGOR: *(Over the letter)* What?

ERNA: Isn't that Dustin Hoffman?

GREGOR: *(Looks up at the television)* Yes.

(They go back to reading the letter.)

Scene Seven

Title: THE LAND OF OPPORTUNITY

(GREGOR sits at the table, writing in a small account book. ERNA sits with her feet up.)

GREGOR: Ninety-seven dollars in the shoes in the closet. One hundred and thirty-seven taped under the bathroom rug. Four hundred and five dollars in the overhead light.

ERNA: If it hasn't burned up.

GREGOR: It hasn't. *(Pause. He gets up, gets a chair, stands on the chair and checks in the overhead light. Getting down:)* It hasn't. *(He sits back at the table.)* Sixty-five dollars under the mattress. Twelve dollars in the refrigerator.

(ERNA laughs.)

GREGOR: What's funny?

ERNA: In Prague we hid our friends' plays, here we hide —. *(She laughs.)*

GREGOR: Why is that funny?

ERNA: Not funny, just ironic, that's all.

GREGOR: To you everything is ironic, isn't it?

ERNA: I wish that were true.

(Pause)

GREGOR: We still have one-thousand, two-hundred and fifty-three dollars left of what my cousin loaned us.

ERNA: Loaned *you*. Don't put me in your cousin's debt. He can hardly keep his hands off me as it is.

GREGOR: What an imagination. Everyone either hates you or is trying to paw you. You're not thirty anymore, Erna.

ERNA: I'm sorry?

GREGOR: Forget it.

ERNA: You said I wasn't thirty anymore.

GREGOR: *(Without looking up)* So?

ERNA: Why did you say that?

(He shrugs.)

ERNA: I suppose you are thirty.

GREGOR: I enjoy being the age I am. I'm not ashamed.

ERNA: And I am?

GREGOR: You're an actress, Erna.

ERNA: What is that supposed to mean?

GREGOR: Look, isn't this a stupid thing to argue about?

ERNA: I didn't realize we were arguing.

GREGOR: We were just about to. Trust me.

(Pause. She moves away.)

GREGOR: One thousand, two-hundred and fifty-three divided by.... I think we'll be fine for another four months.

ERNA: Three.

GREGOR: Three and a half.

ERNA: Three.

GREGOR: Three.

ERNA: Maybe two and a half.

GREGOR: Three, Erna.

(Pause)

ERNA: And then what?

GREGOR: Something will happen. I'm having meetings.

ERNA: Everybody has meetings. I can have meetings.

GREGOR: So have them. *(Short pause)* They've seen my film. They liked it. They told me they liked it. We have three and a half months.

ERNA: Two.

(Short pause)

GREGOR: Look, if nothing works out by then, I'll drive a taxi.

ERNA: You'll drive a taxi?

GREGOR: Yes.

ERNA: You don't know how to drive, Gregor.

GREGOR: I'll learn.

ERNA: You'll learn?

GREGOR: That's right.

ERNA: Of course. Why not? When we left you did say in America everything was possible. Unfortunately I did not understand "everything" to mean you learning to drive a car.

GREGOR: It can't be hard. It's something at least.

ERNA: I guess it is. *(Pause)* I can scrub floors.

GREGOR: You'd do that?

ERNA: Look what I've already done.

GREGOR: "Look what I've already done." I see. New tactic. The martyr. Don't worry, I'm not going to let you scrub floors. *(Short pause)* I'll scrub floors.

ERNA: But what else can an old former actress do?

GREGOR: Erna, you are not a former actress —.

ERNA: But a minute ago you said —.

GREGOR: What I said had nothing to do with your acting. I'm sorry I said anything.

(Pause)

ERNA: Maybe you can get the attaché's chauffeur to teach you how to drive.

(He looks at her.)

ERNA: You could just ask.

(Pause)

GREGOR: I'm not going to ask for an exit stamp, Erna. We've been through this. I'm on their list. Do you know what that means?

ERNA: But if you said the right things.

GREGOR: I've already said the right things, which is why we left.

ERNA: Which is why *you* left. *(Pause)* I left with you. *(Long pause)* Gregor, it is all coming apart.

GREGOR: Nothing is coming apart.

ERNA: Look up.

(She stands over him. He doesn't look up. He has been looking through a small date book.)

GREGOR: I have three meetings today. *(Pause; without looking up)* We have three months.

ERNA: Two and a half. *(She looks away.)*

Scene Eight

Title: BY THE BOOTSTRAPS

(Late evening. GREGOR is at the open window; ERNA is at a distance, watching him. He is drunk.)

GREGOR: *(Shouting out the window)* America, I love you! Do you hear me, America?!

ERNA: I think America's heard enough for one night, Gregor, so you can close the window.

GREGOR: *(Pointing)* America, Erna.

ERNA: Now you tell me. I said close the window. You're drunk.

GREGOR: Yes.

(He moves away from the window. She goes and closes it.)

GREGOR: *(To himself)* Yes. *(He turns to* ERNA.*)* But Erna....

ERNA: Yes, Gregor?

GREGOR: I think I have the right to be drunk.

ERNA: That is definitely just one person's opinion.

GREGOR: Besides, the boy producer was paying. *(He laughs to himself.)* He didn't know shit. Erna, did I tell you he has his own theater in this Hartford and he didn't know shit?

ERNA: Is that what you told the producer, Gregor, that he didn't know shit?

GREGOR: What? Erna, don't be stupid. Even in America you can't be stupid.

ERNA: You figured that out by yourself?

GREGOR: I told him I was grateful! I thanked him for considering me. I was charming. And I was grateful. We all should be. You too, Erna.

ERNA: Leave me out of this, please. Have your own fun. I want to go to bed.

GREGOR: Erna...?

ERNA: Now what, Gregor?

GREGOR: I told you about the play, didn't I? I might be directing this play?

ERNA: Tell me again tomorrow. Get undressed. *(Short pause)* Or maybe you need help?

GREGOR: *(He looks at his clothes, weaves a bit.)* I don't know.

ERNA: *(She goes to undress him.)* Sit down. *(She pushes him down on the couch.)* Pick up your feet. *(He does. She starts to take off his shoes.)*

GREGOR: Erna, we are going to get out of this goddamn one room.

ERNA: Not tonight, Gregor. I'm not going anywhere with you tonight.

GREGOR: But I don't mean tonight.

ERNA: No? Lift your arms. *(He does. She pulls the sweater over his head.)*

GREGOR: Three months. We had only three months. This boy was really impressed with me. As well he should be.

ERNA: Impressed with how much you could drink?

GREGOR: Erna, it's about time we got something, do you understand?

ERNA: What something would you like to get? Another television set?

GREGOR: *(Getting up)* Erna —

ERNA: Stay still.

GREGOR: *(Moving toward the window)* I want you to look at this with me....

ERNA: Gregor, leave that window closed. *(He does.)* And please keep your voice down.

GREGOR: *(He nods and begins to whisper.)* Look at all that. That is here, Erna. We are here. I mean....

(Short pause)

ERNA: What *do* you mean?

(Pause. He looks out the window.)

ERNA: Sit down and I'll take your pants off.

GREGOR: *(Still at the window)* Listen to me! Sh-sh. This is the world today. Like it or not, Erna, understand? *(She sits down.)* This is...culture. Call it shit, Erna. Go ahead. But that's fine. Shit is fine. And we found it. It is ours. We're here.

(He goes and sits next to her. He lifts his legs.)

GREGOR: Take my pants off. *(She begins to.)* I just want to see your attaché friend's face when he hears. I was choked, but I didn't strangle.

ERNA: He's not my friend, Gregor. And besides I doubt if he'll even hear.

GREGOR: Oh they hear. They're probably in the next room hearing right now.

ERNA: Gregor.

GREGOR: Figuratively. Figuratively, Erna.

ERNA: I'll get your pajamas. *(She goes toward the bathroom.)*

GREGOR: Wait! *(He jumps up with his pants around his ankles.)* I want you to understand one thing. One thing you are not understanding, Erna.

ERNA: What is that?

GREGOR: Understand that if a man can achieve something in this world, Erna. Here! In America. Then —.

ERNA: Then what?

GREGOR: Then, he achieves everywhere. Just by achieving here. That's what this is. It's the center.

ERNA: I don't understand.

GREGOR: Wait! If a man's a poet here, Erna. Listen to me!!! He is not a Czech poet here, Erna. He is a poet.

Period. That's what I mean. That's what this is all about.
That's why everyone wants to be here.

(Short pause)

ERNA: Not everyone, Gregor.

GREGOR: Who?! Who?! No one we know, Erna.

(Pause)

ERNA: Here, put your own pajamas on. *(She throws him his pajamas.)*

GREGOR: I can. I can.

(He tries. She picks up a blanket and moves toward the bathroom.)

GREGOR: What are you doing?

ERNA: I'm going to sleep in the bathroom.

GREGOR: Oh.

(She goes into the bathroom, closes the door. He tries to put his pajamas on and falls. She comes out and looks at him.)

GREGOR: I can do it myself!!!

(She goes back into the bathroom and slams the door.)

Scene Nine

Title: SHADOWS

(Evening. GREGOR is at the table, looking through a photo album. Bread on the table. ERNA lights candles.)

ERNA: Where is this Hartford?

GREGOR: *(Without looking up)* In the north. I could take a train. Why didn't you tell me before that you'd brought these photographs?

ERNA: I didn't? *(He looks up.)* I must have been waiting for the right time.

(He smiles, looks back down.)

ERNA: Here's a knife to cut the bread with. *(Gives him the knife)*

GREGOR: *(Looking at a photo)* Vlasta in my LOWER DEPTHS. I haven't thought about Vlasta for years.

ERNA: Vlasta's been dead for years, Gregor.

GREGOR: For years?

(She nods. He shakes his head. Pause.)

ERNA: The food last night with the producer, was it good?

GREGOR: The food?

ERNA: In the restaurant.

GREGOR: Yes, it was very good.

ERNA: Oh. *(Short pause)* Perhaps you're not very hungry then.

GREGOR: *(Without looking up)* I'm hungry.

ERNA: Maybe you ate too much last night.

GREGOR: No, I'm —. *(He looks at her.)* I'm hungry, Erna.

ERNA: Good.

(GREGOR looks back over the album.)

GREGOR: Lukash, Erna.

ERNA: Lukash?

(She goes to him.)

ERNA: Where? *(He points.)* That's Lukash? In THE LOWER DEPTHS? He wasn't in THE LOWER DEPTHS.

GREGOR: This isn't THE LOWER DEPTHS. I can't figure out what this is. It isn't one of mine. But that's Lukash.

ERNA: Yes. That's Lukash. I don't think I saw this play. *(Moves to go back to the kitchen)*

GREGOR: Wait. I remember. It's another Gorky. The one they closed.

ERNA: They closed a Gorky?

GREGOR: In rehearsal they closed it. They're in rehearsal clothes, see? Erna, where did you get these photographs?

ERNA: From friends, Gregor.

(She goes and gets a bottle of wine.)

GREGOR: *(Being shown the bottle)* What is this?

ERNA: Will you open it?

GREGOR: Czech wine? Erna, where did you find Czech wine?

ERNA: In the store. Just open it, please.

GREGOR: You asked for Czech wine?

ERNA: Why not?

(She goes and gets a cigarette; GREGOR smiles to himself, and shakes his head. He looks back at the album as ERNA holds up a large book.)

ERNA: Gregor...?

GREGOR: *(Looking up)* What is it?

ERNA: I borrowed it from the library.

GREGOR: You went to the library? When?

ERNA: *(Reading the title)* "PHOTOGRAPHS OF PRAGUE." I thought you might....

GREGOR: *(Smiling)* Yes.

(She sets the book back down.)

GREGOR: Thank you. Why don't you sit down.

ERNA: In a minute. I want to put in the pie.

(She goes to the oven.)

GREGOR: You're making a pie? *(Short pause)* Erna, I think you're trying to seduce me.

ERNA: Think whatever you want. I'm making a pie.

(Pause. She puts the pie into the oven.)

GREGOR: *(Looking over the album)* Erna, your THREE SISTERS.

ERNA: My Olga? *(Goes to him)*

GREGOR: No. Your Irina, I think.

ERNA: Yes. That's my Irina. Gregor, these are old.

GREGOR: Very old.

ERNA: Not that old.

(She moves back to the oven.)

GREGOR: Pavek as Sganarelle.

ERNA: Pavek? Really? *(She wipes her hands and goes to see.)*

GREGOR: Why are you so interested in Pavek?

ERNA: I liked Pavek.

GREGOR: I didn't know that.

ERNA: You knew I liked Pavek.

GREGOR: No. I didn't know. When did you like him?

ERNA: Gregor, I only liked him. He was a great actor.

GREGOR: I see.

ERNA: Gregor — Pavek was a homosexual. We were friends.

GREGOR: Pavek? You know you shouldn't say that.

ERNA: Gregor, I can say it here.

GREGOR: I suppose so. *(Short pause)* Pavek a homosexual? I didn't know.

ERNA: That's why he killed himself.

GREGOR: I thought he killed himself because of gambling. That's what we all thought.

ERNA: I know that's what everyone thought. But he didn't gamble, Gregor. He was caught. He didn't want his daughter to know. He killed himself.

GREGOR: You knew this?

ERNA: We talked. If he killed himself there wouldn't be a trial. And his son-in-law could keep his job as a foreman. They made it all very clear to him.

GREGOR: He told you all this?

ERNA: Yes.

GREGOR: What did you say to him?

ERNA: What could I say?

GREGOR: Then you knew he was going to kill himself?

ERNA: I knew he was thinking about it. I told him to emigrate.

GREGOR: He wouldn't do that.

ERNA: No.

GREGOR: Not with his son-in-law being a foreman. He'd never be able to live with himself. He was too sensitive.

ERNA: He was very sensitive. *(Looks at the album)* That's not Pavek.

GREGOR: That's Marek as Don Juan. See that shadow—

ERNA: Yes.

GREGOR: That's Pavek.

ERNA: The shadow?

GREGOR: Can't you tell?

ERNA: Yes. That's Pavek. Of course.

GREGOR: He was a lovely man. Beautiful.

ERNA: His daughter was lovely too.

GREGOR: He lived for her. How was he caught?

ERNA: In the train station.

GREGOR: I didn't know that. They kept it all very quiet. Usually something like that everyone knows.

ERNA: Everyone didn't know. That's why he had to shoot himself.

(Pause. GREGOR looks at more photos.)

GREGOR: I can't figure out where you got all these. Half of them I've never seen before.

ERNA: *(Going back into the kitchen)* I had them.

GREGOR: With you? At home?

ERNA: I collected them from our friends.

GREGOR: Oh.

ERNA: Before we left.

GREGOR: Oh. Well it's nice to have something to remember Prague by.

ERNA: We have many things to remember Prague by, Gregor.

(Pause. GREGOR laughs.)

ERNA: What?

GREGOR: Bruz in the Feydeau.

(Without looking at the picture, she laughs too. He turns to another page.)

ERNA: So you will be gone how long?

GREGOR: Five weeks. If I go.

ERNA: If? I thought —

GREGOR: I haven't been given a contract yet.

ERNA: Huh.

GREGOR: What does that mean?

ERNA: It means — huh.

(Pause)

GREGOR: *(Over the album)* Look at Vanek's set for THE CHERRY ORCHARD, Erna.

(She goes and looks and then moves back to the kitchen.)

ERNA: We could write Vanek. He's in Paris, isn't he?

GREGOR: No.

ERNA: He's not in Paris?

GREGOR: You know as well as I know that Vanek went back, Erna.

ERNA: I forgot.

GREGOR: *(Without looking at her)* No you didn't.

(Pause)

ERNA: And in this Hartford, they have good sets?

GREGOR: I don't know.

ERNA: But you said you saw pictures.

GREGOR: I saw plans. For the stage. I didn't see pictures.

ERNA: They didn't show you pictures?

GREGOR: No. *(Short pause)* It's a highly regarded theater, Erna.

(Pause)

ERNA: I just don't know how they put on plays in America in just five weeks.

GREGOR: I'd rather not talk about it. I don't want to get my hopes up.

ERNA: No. You don't.

GREGOR: Even if I don't get the job, we should at least be pleased that people are beginning to think of me.

ERNA: A lot of people think of you, Gregor.

(Pause. She goes back to the kitchen. Then, noticing the expression on his face:)

ERNA: What's wrong?

GREGOR: *(Holding some loose photos)* What is this?

ERNA: What?

GREGOR: These pictures.

ERNA: *(Over his shoulder)* I don't know.

GREGOR: Who gave these to you?

ERNA: Those? I don't remember.

GREGOR: Did Marek give them to you?

ERNA: Most of our friends gave me pictures, Gregor. What are they of?

GREGOR: Marek's party he gave for me.

ERNA: I wasn't there.

GREGOR: I know you weren't there. I remember everyone who was there. There were five of us. And no one was taking pictures. No one would at a party like that.

ERNA: Obviously someone took pictures. There they are.

GREGOR: This is a joke.

ERNA: What is?

GREGOR: Erna, what I said at that party is what I was denounced for.

ERNA: Gregor —!

GREGOR: What I said to the officials later didn't help. But what I said at that party was the start.

ERNA: They are dark. Gregor, I didn't know.

GREGOR: This is someone's idea of a joke.

ERNA: It's a sick joke, Gregor.

GREGOR: When you asked our friends for pictures, did you say why?

ERNA: No. But I'm sure they knew.

GREGOR: Yes.

ERNA: They could see it in our faces.

GREGOR: Yes.

ERNA: We could always see it in someone's face before he left. *(Pause. She sits.)* Marek gave me some. Also Bruz. Jaroslav —.

GREGOR: Jaroslav. I never did trust Jaroslav.

ERNA: He denounced you?

GREGOR: I don't know. *(Short pause)* I don't know. *(Short pause)* In any case, it doesn't matter now.

ERNA: No?

(Pause)

GREGOR: Blow out the candles. I want to turn on some lights, it's dark in here.

(She blows out the candles.)

Scene Ten

Title: THE FREE WORLD

(GREGOR *sits.* ERNA *is in the kitchen. She takes a kettle, fills it with water, places it on the stove.*)

GREGOR: So you won't go?

(*She shrugs.*)

GREGOR: It's ten to twelve. The producer said he'd see you at twelve.

ERNA: I never said I would, Gregor.

GREGOR: But I thought....

ERNA: Then maybe you thought wrong.

GREGOR: Yes. I'll call him later and apologize for you not showing up.

ERNA: I don't want you apologizing for me.

GREGOR: You don't leave me any choice, Erna.

ERNA: So now I'm hurting you.

GREGOR: You're not hurting me. I don't care what you do.

ERNA: Is that true?

GREGOR: It's a free world here, do what you want.

ERNA: You don't want that, Gregor.

GREGOR: I wouldn't bet on that.

(*Pause. They look at each other.*)

GREGOR: It wasn't much of a part. And who knows if you'd even have gotten it. It was only an audition.

ERNA: I'd have gotten it.

GREGOR: How do you know? You don't know how things are done here.

ERNA: I know because my husband is directing the play.

GREGOR: Erna, is that why —?

ERNA: I don't know! *(Short pause)* Please, just leave me alone for now.

(He nods and stands up.)

ERNA: Where are you going?

GREGOR: You just said you wanted me to leave you alone.

ERNA: That doesn't mean I don't want to know where you're going.

GREGOR: I'm going to take a shower. *(He moves to the bathroom.)* Josef's coming by. Let him in when he buzzes.

ERNA: Josef's coming by?

GREGOR: I asked him over when I thought you'd be out.

ERNA: Josef can come when I'm here.

GREGOR: He doesn't speak Czech, Erna. You'd have to speak English. I didn't know if you were ready for that.

(He goes into the bathroom.)

ERNA: Gregor —!

(He closes the door. After a moment we hear the shower turned on. ERNA throws herself on the couch, after turning on the television. Pause. Suddenly she sits up, looks at her watch, gets up, and puts her coat on. She calls:)

ERNA: Gregor, will you call the producer and tell him I'll be late?!!

GREGOR: *(Off)* I can't hear you, Erna!

ERNA: I said, call the —.

(Buzzer sounds.)

ERNA: Gregor, I think it's —.

GREGOR: *(Off)* Is that Josef?

ERNA: Gregor?!

GREGOR: *(Off)* Push the button, Erna! He's downstairs!

(She picks up the buzzer/phone.)

ERNA: HELLO? HELLO? *(She pushes buttons.)* Gregor, no one is —.

(The water boils, the kettles whistles. Into the phone:)

ERNA: JUST A —.

(The telephone rings. In a bit of a panic:)

ERNA: Gregor!!

(Phone rings.)

GREGOR: *(Off)* Answer the phone!!

(She hurries to the phone; the kettle is whistling, television is on. On her way she knocks over a glass.)

ERNA: *(Into phone)* HELLO? I AM SORRY?

GREGOR: *(Off)* Was that Josef?

ERNA: *(Into phone)* WHAT? I DO NOT —.

(Knock at the door)

ERNA: Just a minute. ONE MOMENT PLEASE. *(Into phone)* Can you speak to my husband? I AM SORRY, I WAS SPEAKING CZECH. I SAID, CAN YOU —.

GREGOR: *(Off)* What are you doing out there?! Let him in, Erna!

ERNA: *(Into phone)* HELLO? I DO NOT UNDERSTAND, MISTER —.

(Another knock; she calls back:)

ERNA: I DO COME! *(Into phone)* IF I BUY MAGAZINES
I WIN FREE TRIP TO THIS MIAMI BEACH????

(Television, whistling kettle, knocking. GREGOR *comes out in
his robe.)*

GREGOR: *(Yells)* Erna!!!

ERNA: *(Pleading)* Gregor!

Scene Eleven

Title: GOING PLACES

*(*ERNA *sits at the table. In front of her is an English grammar
book. As she practices she covers with one hand the line she is
supposed to figure out.)*

ERNA: I WILL GO TO THE PARK.
I GO TO THE PARK.
I HAVE...GONE TO THE PARK.
I... *(Checks)* WENT? What is this WENT? *(Short pause)*
HE WILL GO TO THE SCHOOL.
HE GOES TO THE SCHOOL.
HE HAS GONE TO THE SCHOOL.
HE WENT TO THE SCHOOL. *(Short pause)*
SHE...WILL GO TO THE REFRIGERATOR.
(She gets up and moves to the refrigerator.)
SHE GOES TO THE REFRIGERATOR.
*(She opens the refrigerator door, looks, closes it without
finding anything she wants.)*
SHE HAS GONE TO THE REFRIGERATOR.
(She sits back at the table.)
SHE WENT TO THE REFRIGERATOR.
(Continues with the book:)
YOU WILL GO TO THE POST OFFICE.
YOU GO TO THE POST OFFICE.
YOU HAVE GONE TO THE POST OFFICE.
YOU WENT TO THE POST OFFICE. *(Short pause)*

WE WILL GO TO THE CITY.
WE GO TO THE CITY.
WE HAVE GONE.... *(She stops. Pause.)*
(Quietly, looking up) WE WILL GO...HOME.
WE GO...HOME.
WE HAVE GONE...HOME.
WE WENT...HOME. *(Pause)*

Scene Twelve

Title: SIBERIA

(ERNA is ironing. GREGOR sits, writing down something on a small piece of paper. He has a pile of books in front of him.)

(Pause. He gets up.)

GREGOR: Here's the phone numbers for the theater and my hotel.

(He holds it out. She nods, but doesn't look at him or take the paper.)

GREGOR: I'll set it on the table. *(She nods.)*

(Pause)

GREGOR: You are going to be all right, aren't you?

ERNA: Of course. Why wouldn't I be all right? What time was your train?

GREGOR: I have an hour.

(He goes back to sorting through the books, trying to decide what to take.)

ERNA: If you end up needing one of those, I can mail it to you.

GREGOR: Thank you. *(Short pause)* You're going to wear that shirt out — if you keep ironing it.

ERNA: *(Shrugs)* I want you to look nice.... I think Americans judge you by how you look.

GREGOR: Since when, Erna?

ERNA: It's not true?

GREGOR: If you'd seen the producer of the theater — I doubt if he's worn an ironed shirt all his adult life.

ERNA: But he's still a boy. The boys can dress like that. You're not a boy anymore, Gregor.

GREGOR: If you're only worried about how I *look*, then why have you been up since five pressing my underwear?

(Short pause)

ERNA: I just wanted to.

(He smiles. She finishes ironing, folds the shirt, and puts it in the suitcase. He writes something.)

GREGOR: Here, you'll need the address of the theater if you're going to send anything. *(She doesn't look at him.)* I'll put it with the phone numbers. *(He does. Pause.)* I asked Josef to look in on you. *(She nods.)* Maybe the two of you can go to a show.

(Pause)

ERNA: Maybe.

(Pause)

GREGOR: After all, it's only five weeks, Erna. And then you'll come to Hartford for the opening.

ERNA: I'll never understand how Americans can rehearse their plays in only five weeks.

(Pause)

GREGOR: You will come up for the opening, won't you?

ERNA: I might be going to a show that night with Josef.

*(He smiles. He packs some books in a bag. Long pause. She
closes the suitcase.)*

ERNA: There's instant coffee in the bag. And I made you
a lunch — cheese and salami. It's in the refrigerator. I'll
get it. *(She does.)* And there's toilet paper —.

GREGOR: I think the hotel will have toilet paper.

ERNA: *(Ignoring him)* And I packed the clock —.

GREGOR: What will you use?

ERNA: You can figure out the time by watching the
television. There's two bars of soap with the toilet
paper, and your coat brush.

GREGOR: I'll be sure to brush off the blond hairs before I
come home.

(ERNA looks up at him, then smiles.)

ERNA: And two cartons of cigarettes. The matches I
stuffed in your slippers —.

GREGOR: Erna, I'm not going to Siberia.

(Long pause)

ERNA: Help me put the ironing board away.

*(He does. They set it in the kitchen area. He takes her hand.
She tries not to cry.)*

GREGOR: Erna....

(He hugs her, she hugs back. Pause. Then lights fade.)

Scene Thirteen

Title: HIS MEMORY

*(This scene is GREGOR's memory of their first moments in
the apartment. Stage empty. Door opens, GREGOR then
ERNA enter with suitcases.)*

GREGOR: HELLO? IS SOMEONE IN HERE PLEASE? *(To* ERNA*)* No one's here.

(They look around.)

ERNA: *(Pointing to the door buzzer)* What is this?

GREGOR: To let people in the front door. *(Noticing something on the table)* She left a note. *(He reads.)* "DEAR MR. AND MRS. HASEK. SORRY I COULDN'T WELCOME YOU MYSELF, BUT BUSINESS IN L.A. CALLS."

ERNA: What is 'L.A.'?

GREGOR: Los Angeles. *(Continues to read)* "ENJOY THE SUBLET. FEEL FREE TO USE ANYTHING HERE. AND IF YOU HAVE ANY QUESTIONS JUST CALL THE SUPER."

ERNA: What is this 'SUPER?'

GREGOR: It's nice, don't you think?

ERNA: Is that the bedroom?

GREGOR: *(Opens a door)* A closet. I don't think there is a bedroom. The couch folds out.

ERNA: I see. *(She opens her bag for a cigarette, then notices.)* Gregor — the refrigerator!

GREGOR: My God.

ERNA: Why is it so big?

GREGOR: I don't know. *(He opens it.)* Erna, she left a bottle of vodka for us.

ERNA: It's not for us, Gregor.

GREGOR: Of course it's for us. Look in the cabinets for some glasses.

ERNA: I don't think we should, Gregor.

GREGOR: There are a couple here in the sink.

(He opens the vodka.)

ERNA: Gregor, it's not ours.

(He hands her a glass.)

GREGOR: *(Toasts)* To our new home.

Scene Fourteen

Title: HER MEMORY

(This scene is ERNA's *memory of their first moments in the apartment. As in the previous scene,* ERNA *and* GREGOR *with suitcases;* GREGOR *has found the note.)*

GREGOR: *(Reading)* "DEAR MR. AND MRS. HASEK. SORRY I COULDN'T WELCOME YOU MYSELF, BUT BUSINESS IN L.A. CALLS. *(To* ERNA*)* What is 'L.A.'? *(She shrugs.)* *(Reading)* "I'M SURE YOU WILL TREAT MY HOME AS IF IT WERE YOURS. ANY PROBLEMS JUST CALL THE SUPER."

ERNA: Call what?

GREGOR: *(Shrugs)* I don't know.

ERNA: *(Pointing to the buzzer)* What is this?

GREGOR: *(Shrugs)* To call the concierge? I don't think there's a bedroom.

ERNA: Maybe the couch folds out. Gregor — the refrigerator!

GREGOR: What do you need a refrigerator that big for?

(They look at each other. GREGOR *opens the refrigerator.)*

GREGOR: There's some vodka. *(Short pause)* Do you think we should...?

ERNA: I don't know, Gregor?

GREGOR: She left it in the refrigerator.

ERNA: I wouldn't.

GREGOR: Maybe just a little, she'll never know.

(He takes two glasses out of the sink. Pause.)

ERNA: What's wrong?

GREGOR: I'm just tired.

ERNA: Come here.

(She takes him by the hand.)

GREGOR: *(Scared)* Well, we made it. To us??

(She nods. They drink.)

GREGOR: Don't you want to take off your coat?

ERNA: I'm not ready yet. Everything's still too new.

GREGOR: It's nice, isn't it? *(She holds him around the waist.)* Isn't it? *(He looks out the window.)* Erna...?

ERNA: What?

GREGOR: Look at those buildings. They're very tall, aren't they?

ERNA: *(Nods)* Gregor, let's try not to be scared.

(Pause)

GREGOR: We will try again here.

ERNA: We have each other, Gregor.

(They hug.)

Scene Fifteen

Title: SIBERIA CONTINUED

(The same as at the end of Scene Twelve. They are hugging. ERNA slips something into GREGOR's hand.)

GREGOR: What's this?

ERNA: Don't look at it now.

(She moves away to get his coat.)

GREGOR: A picture? Of you?

ERNA: Look at it on the train.

(She helps him put on his coat.)

GREGOR: Thank you. *(Short pause)* Erna, what's left in the refrigerator for you?

ERNA: Plenty. Don't worry.

(He nods. He picks up his bags.)

GREGOR: I'll call when I get there. *(She nods.)* You take care. Please.

(She nods. He hesitates.)

ERNA: You're going to miss your train.

(He kisses her on the cheek.)

ERNA: Will you go, I want to wash the dishes.

(He smiles. Nods. And slowly leaves. She closes the door behind him. She sighs, almost shaking now. She goes into the kitchen,turns the water on, then suddenly hurries to the window, leaving the water running. She watches out the window and then sees him.)

ERNA: Look up. Look up! Look —.

(She waves — he has looked up. She smiles, watches him walk down the street, turns back to the room, sits. She takes out a cigarette. She gets up and locks the chain lock on the door. She goes back and sits. The water runs.)

Scene Sixteen

Title: A FEW DAYS BEFORE

(Rain on the window. GREGOR, *on the couch, in his robe, a thermometer in his mouth.* ERNA *is in the kitchen taking groceries out of a bag. She has just come in and still wears her coat.)*

(Pause. Then GREGOR *takes out the thermometer and looks at it, then he shakes it.* ERNA *watches this. He senses this and turns to her.)*

GREGOR: I'm fine. *(Short pause)* I'll soon be fine.

(Pause)

ERNA: *(While unpacking)* I'll go to the pharmacy; what you need is a little camphor oil.

GREGOR: You just came back. It's raining.

ERNA: If you're going to Hartford you can't be sick.

GREGOR: "If"?

(Short pause)

ERNA: When. When. I'll put hot water on for tea and then I'll go.

GREGOR: Erna....

ERNA: *(Takes a newspaper out of the bag)* Here's the paper if you want it. *(She goes to the couch to hand it to him.)*

GREGOR: Erna. *(He grabs her.)*

ERNA: I'll just be gone a minute, Gregor. I'm not deserting you. *(Notices his expression)* What?

(He reaches under a cushion and takes out a large envelope.)

GREGOR: *(As he takes out a newspaper clipping and a letter)* This came. From my cousin. Skreta wrote him and offered me two productions for the season. This was enclosed.

(Shows her the newspaper clipping.)

GREGOR: The party paper. It's a summary of my career in the party paper. *(Reads)* "Gregor Hasek, Director of extraordinary vision." *(Short pause)* They praise me. I leave the country and they praise me.

(ERNA takes the paper and begins to read.)

GREGOR: At the end of the article they say I've been sick for the past months. I'm resting by the Black Sea.

ERNA: You're by the Black Sea?

GREGOR: That's what they say. *(Short pause)* I've been sick.

(Short pause, then suddenly they both laugh, and shake their heads. ERNA continues to read, sitting now on the couch. GREGOR gets up and goes into the kitchen. As he makes himself an instant coffee he watches ERNA as she reads.)

GREGOR: *(Finally)* Skreta could protect me.

ERNA: No one can protect you.

GREGOR: No.

(Pause)

ERNA: *(Turns to look at him)* But if anyone could, it would be Skreta.

GREGOR: True.

ERNA: *(More to herself)* Two productions.

GREGOR: *(As he stirs his coffee)* Do you think we should go back?

ERNA: *(Excited, she stands and goes to get a cigarette from her purse.)* I try not to think anymore.

(She goes back to the couch. Pause. Neither looks at the other.)

GREGOR: Maybe we should.

ERNA: You don't want that. You have your career in Hartford to think about now. *(She turns to him; he is holding his face and shaking.)* Why are you shaking?

GREGOR: I'm sick. I'm by the Black Sea. *(Short pause)* Wouldn't it make you happy?

ERNA: To be by the Black Sea? I never liked the Black Sea, Gregor. *(He turns and stares at her.)* I wouldn't mind the mountains, Gregor.

GREGOR: Just tell me what is right. I want to know what will make you happy.

ERNA: Are those now the same question?

GREGOR: Erna —.

ERNA: Are those now the same question, Gregor?!!

GREGOR: I want what you want!

ERNA: That's not true! That's never been true! *(Beat)* Sometimes it's been true.

GREGOR: I want you to get better!

ERNA: I'm not the one who's sick. I'm not the one who is sick, you understand that, don't you?!

GREGOR: *(Pointing to the newspaper clipping)* To tell you the truth I thought you'd be overjoyed.

ERNA: You won't go.

GREGOR: I would — for you.

ERNA: I don't want you to go — for me.

GREGOR: Can't I do something for you?! Can you only do things for me?!!!

(Long pause)

ERNA: *(Quietly)* Then let's go home.

GREGOR: Fine.

ERNA: When?

GREGOR: Whenever. *(Nods to her)*

(ERNA suddenly gets up and goes to the closet.)

GREGOR: What are you doing?

ERNA: I'm packing.

GREGOR: So it really is what you want.

ERNA: It is.

GREGOR: We just leave?

ERNA: That's right.

GREGOR: You really want me to do that.

ERNA: Yes, I do.

GREGOR: *(Yells)* You would do that to me?!!

ERNA: Gregor??

GREGOR: I thought you loved me. *(He shakes his head, moves toward the bathroom, then suddenly turns back)* Did you hear what I said?!! I thought you loved me!!

(He goes into the bathroom, slamming the door.)

ERNA: Gregor??

Scene Seventeen

Title: ERNA RECALLS AN EARLIER SCENE

(Morning, weeks earlier. ERNA stands by the window with an English-language copy of Chekhov's THREE SISTERS in her hand. GREGOR, in his robe, sits on the couch; he smokes,

drinks coffee. In front of him is another copy of THREE SISTERS, which he is following.)

(Pause)

GREGOR: *(Lighting a cigarette)* Whenever you're ready.

(She nods.)

ERNA: *(Reads)* "ONE YEAR AGO ON THIS VERY DAY, MAY FIFTH —"

GREGOR: *(Correcting her pronounciation, as he does throughout the scene)* FIFTH. MAY FIFTH, Erna.

ERNA: "MAY FIFTH — ON YOUR BIRTHDAY, IRINA — FATHER DIED. IT WAS BITTER COLD AND SNOWING."

GREGOR: COLD. AND. I'm not hearing the 'd's.

ERNA: COLD. AND. "AT THE TIME, IT ALL SEEMED MORE THAN I COULD BEAR; YOU FAINTED, I EVEN THOUGHT YOU HAD DIED."

GREGOR: "I EVEN THOUGHT YOU HAD DIED."

ERNA: "I EVEN THOUGHT YOU HAD DIED."

GREGOR: It's one phrase. "I EVEN THOUGHT YOU HAD DIED."

ERNA: "I EVEN THOUGHT YOU HAD DIED." *(Continues)* "IT'S BEEN ONLY A YEAR, WE CAN BARELY REMEMBER IT. YOU'RE BACK WEARING WHITE; YOUR FACE GLOWS."

GREGOR: It's — "WEARING WHITE."

ERNA: "...WEARING WHITE; YOUR FACE GLOWS."

GREGOR: *(Taking a sip of coffee)* Bong. Bong. Bong.

ERNA: "THE CLOCK STRUCK THEN TOO."

GREGOR: You should turn to the clock. See the clock.

ERNA: See the clock?

GREGOR: Yes.

ERNA: I should turn and see the clock here?

GREGOR: Yes.

ERNA: I never turn to see the clock here. Two hundred performances of THREE SISTERS and I have never turned here. Olga doesn't move here.

GREGOR: It's better if she turns. In my production she turned.

ERNA: In our production she didn't, Gregor. Skreta didn't want me to turn. You must have seen that production twenty times, why didn't you ever say anything before?

GREGOR: Skreta was the director, Erna. Just try it, you'll see.

ERNA: I'll see what?

GREGOR: That I'm right.

ERNA: So I should turn here.

GREGOR: Yes.

ERNA: Why?

GREGOR: Why?... I don't remember why, Erna. My production was ten years ago. I just remember it worked. And that's what we're after.

ERNA: That it works? That's not what we're after, Gregor.

GREGOR: Will you just try it?

(Pause)

ERNA: *(Reading)* "IT'S BEEN ONLY A YEAR, WE CAN BARELY REMEMBER IT. YOU'RE BACK WEARING WHITE —"

GREGOR: "WHITE," Erna.

ERNA: "—WHITE; YOUR FACE GLOWS."

GREGOR: *(As the clock)* Bong. Bong. Bong.

ERNA: *(Turns)* "THE CLOCK STRUCK THEN TOO."
(Short pause) I turned.

GREGOR: And?

ERNA: And I don't like it. I shouldn't turn there. I never
did.

GREGOR: Fine, then just forget it. Forget I said anything!
Forget I'm even here! What do I care, it's your audition.

ERNA: It's not my audition, Gregor. I never said I was
going to audition. I said I wanted to practice in case I
started to think like I might go to the audition, Gregor.

GREGOR: Whatever you say. Though I seem to recall
that it was you who asked me to help.

ERNA: To help with my English. I don't need direction. I
had a director. Skreta directed me.

GREGOR: And Skreta's a fine director.

(Short pause)

ERNA: So I'm not turning here?

GREGOR: Ask Skreta.

(Short pause)

ERNA: *(Continues)* "I REMEMBER THEM CARRYING
FATHER AWAY."

GREGOR: *(A little hostile now)* "FATHER!" With a 'TH'!

ERNA: "I REMEMBER THEM CARRYING FATHER
AWAY." In the Czech it's different. In the Czech it's
"taking Father out of our house."

GREGOR: Then say that.

ERNA: But it says in the English —.

GREGOR: Say what you want to say, Erna.

ERNA: I want to say what Chekhov wanted.

GREGOR: I don't think Chekhov's going to be at the audition, Erna. But if he is, we'll ask him what he likes.

(She looks at him. Pause.)

ERNA: "I REMEMBER THEM CARRYING FATHER AWAY. THE BAND...." *(To* GREGOR*)* BAND???

GREGOR: You know what it means.

(She mimes a horn player.)

GREGOR: Keep going.

ERNA: "THE BAND PLAYED A MARCH, THEY FIRED RIFLE SHOTS OVER THE GRAVE. FOR A GENERAL OF THE BRIGADE THERE WEREN'T MANY MOURNERS...." Correct me whenever you want, Gregor.

(He says nothing.)

ERNA: "...THERE WEREN'T MANY MOURNERS. WELL, IT WAS RAINING HARD, RAIN MIXED WITH SNOW." Here I turn my head.

(She does; GREGOR *snickers.)*

ERNA: What's funny about that?

GREGOR: Don't ask me, I'm not the director.

(Pause)

ERNA: Here Irina says —

GREGOR: *(Reads)* "WHY THINK ABOUT IT?"

ERNA: That's all?

GREGOR: That's all.

ERNA: In the Czech it's much longer. *(Shakes her head)* Language. *(Continues reading)* "NOW TODAY IT'S

WARM. WE CAN EVEN KEEP THE WINDOWS
OPEN. THOUGH THERE STILL AREN'T ANY
LEAVES ON THE BIRCHES...." *(She gets a small smile on
her face and looks out the window.)* This is true, no leaves
on any birches out there.

(GREGOR just looks at her.)

ERNA: *(Continues)* "...ON THE BIRCHES. IT'S BEEN
ELEVEN YEARS SINCE FATHER WAS PUT IN
CHARGE OF THE BRIGADE—."

GREGOR: *(Without looking up)* "BRIGADE."

ERNA: "...BRIGADE AND WE ALL HAD TO LEAVE
MOSCOW."

GREGOR: "AND WE ALL HAD TO LEAVE MOSCOW."
It's all one sentence.

ERNA: "AND WE ALL HAD TO LEAVE MOSCOW. I
REMEMBER WELL, THAT AT THIS TIME, IN EARLY
MAY, THE SUN BATHES EVERYTHING."

GREGOR: It's BATHES, Erna. BATHES.

ERNA: BATHES.

GREGOR: BATHES. BATHES! Goddamnit!!

ERNA: What's wrong with you?

(He gets up with the book and moves away.)

ERNA: *(Continues)* "AFTER ELEVEN YEARS, I
REMEMBER IT ALL AS IF IT WERE YESTERDAY."

GREGOR: *(Quietly)* "YESTERDAY."

ERNA: "YESTERDAY. OH GOD WHEN I WOKE UP
THIS MORNING AND SAW THE SUNSHINE —"

GREGOR: *(Pacing without looking at her)* SUNSHINE.
SUNSHINE.

ERNA: "SUNSHINE, THAT GOLDEN LIGHT —"

GREGOR: *(Almost shouting now)* THAT GOLDEN LIGHT.

ERNA: "— AND SMELLED —"

GREGOR: SMELLED!!!

ERNA: "— SMELLED —"

GREGOR: *(Reading from his book)* "— SMELLED THE SPRING COMING...."

ERNA: "— SMELLED THE SPRING COMING —."

GREGOR: "— IT MADE ME SO HAPPY...."

ERNA: "— IT MADE ME SO HAPPY —"

GREGOR: Say it right — "— IT MADE ME SO HAPPY...."

ERNA: "— IT MADE ME SO HAPPY —." Gregor, I'm trying.

GREGOR: Then try harder.

ERNA: You mean as hard as you try?!

GREGOR: Once I want to hear it right — "— IT MADE ME SO HAPPY, I LONGED TO GO HOME."

ERNA: "— IT MADE ME SO HAPPY, I LONGED TO GO HOME."

GREGOR: Say it — "I LONG TO GO HOME." "I LONG TO GO HOME."!!!

ERNA: *(Screaming)* "I LONG TO GO HOME." "I LONG TO GO HOME." "I LONG TO GO HOME!!!!!"

(She throws her book at him. Long pause. ERNA looks out the window. GREGOR looks away.)

ERNA: *(More to herself than to GREGOR, she continues Olga's speech from THREE SISTERS, in Czech.)* "Every morning it's school, every afternoon and night there's tutoring. It's no wonder I get those headaches. I have started to think like an old woman. Really, after four years of this work —."

GREGOR: *(Quietly)* In English, Erna.

ERNA: "— it feels as if day after day all my strength, my youth is being drained out of me, squeezed, drop by drop. All that grows inside me now is that longing —"

GREGOR: In English!

ERNA: "— to go to Moscow! Sell the house, leave everything, and to Moscow!"

GREGOR: *(Screaming)*	ERNA: *(Shouting)*
In English!	To Moscow!
In English!	To Moscow!
In English!	To Moscow!

Scene Eighteen

Title: THE CULMINATION ENDS

(We are in the last few moments of Scene One.)

ERNA: I'd better pack.

GREGOR: You'll come to Hartford? *(Pause)* When?

ERNA: I'd better pack.

GREGOR: Come tomorrow. There's a train at ten. I'll make sure someone meets you. I'll talk to the stage manager. Erna....

(She has turned away.)

GREGOR: It'll make us both feel better, I'm sure of it.

(He puts his coat on, goes to kiss her — she doesn't respond.)

ERNA: I'm glad you're sure of it.

GREGOR: *(At the door)* We'll go out to eat. What kind of food would you like? There's a very good Japanese restaurant near the theater....

ERNA: Japanese? Yes. That would make sense for two Czechs in America.

(He goes. She turns the television back on.)

TELEVISION: "The opposition Social Democratic Party, ignoring an appeal by former Chancellor Helmut Schmidt, said today that it could not accept the deployment of American medium-range missiles in West Germany. The decision, taken at a special party congress in Cologne, was the culmination of —"

(The door opens; GREGOR is in the doorway.)

"— a left-wing rebellion against Mr. Schmidt's support for NATO's deployment decision, which contributed to the collapse of his government last year. A resolution adopted by the Social Democrats opposed the deployment of Pershing 2 and cruise missiles, demanded that the United States and the Soviet Union continue their deadlocked arms talks in Geneva, and called on the Soviet Union to reduce its armory of SS-20 missiles targeted on Western Europe. A two-way debate and a vote —."

(GREGOR enters the room and turns off the television.)

ERNA: *(Without looking at him)* Have you come back to give me the name of a good doctor?

(She smiles to herself, gets up, and gets a cigarette. He shakes his head. Pause.)

GREGOR: Why are we lying to each other?

ERNA: I haven't lied. I said I would pack —.

GREGOR: *(Suddenly turns to her)* Did they pay for your plane ticket?

(She nods. He takes out his wallet, opens it, and takes out a number of bills.) Here —!

ERNA: *(Protesting)* Gregor —!

GREGOR: *(Throwing the money down, yells)* Give it to your sister then!! *(Pause. He goes into the kitchen area, leans on the counter, and rubs his face.)* They pay me thirty-five dollars a day for meals. But I have sandwiches in my room. I bought a hot coil so I make my own coffee now in the morning.

ERNA: Aren't you smart to do that.

GREGOR: I'll make half my salary again that way.

ERNA: Not if you start throwing it away on women like my sister.

(She looks at him, he turns away, shaking his head, trying not to smile.)

GREGOR: You'll miss my interview. One of the Hartford papers wants to interview your husband, Erna. There will be a photo as well. *(Short pause)* I could see if they'd use one of both of us.

ERNA: *(Disgusted)* Oh God, Gregor!

(Pause. GREGOR rubs his eyes and sighs.)

ERNA: You know you could still —.

GREGOR: I know! I know, but....

(Pause)

ERNA: Perhaps in time.

GREGOR: No. No. *(Short pause)* Perhaps. *(Pause; without looking up)* They all call me just 'Gregor.' No one even asked. I like that. Even the black at the stage door calls me 'Gregor.' I'm treated.... *(Looks up)* That may seem like nothing to you —.

ERNA: No. It doesn't seem like nothing to me.

(Pause)

GREGOR: I will never look at another woman, Erna.

ERNA: *(Smiles)* This is not the first time you have made me this promise.

GREGOR: When? When did I —?

ERNA: Sophia.

GREGOR: She meant nothing to me. I didn't marry her, Erna.

ERNA: No. No, you didn't. *(Pause. Realizing the time:)* Gregor, the —!

GREGOR: I'll catch a later train.

(ERNA sits, GREGOR stands; they say nothing.)

Scene Nineteen

Title: BETWEEN EAST AND WEST

(GREGOR, alone, sits watching television.)

TELEVISION: "The West German Bundestag, ignoring street demonstrations and warnings from Moscow, voted to proceed with the stationing of American-made, medium-range missiles —"

(GREGOR stands and moves toward the television.)

"— When this was almost immediately followed by the arrival of the first nine of 108 Pershing 2's, Moscow broke off the negotiations in Geneva indefinitely, then announced its own deployment —."

(GREGOR turns the sound down. He goes to the phone.)

GREGOR: *(Into the phone)* I WISH TO MAKE A PHONE CALL TO PRAGUE, CZECHOSLOVAKIA, PLEASE. THANK YOU. *(Pause)* YES. PRAGUE. CZECHOSLOVAKIA. THE NUMBER 86-491. 212-555-5312. THANK YOU.

*(He hangs up. He goes into the kitchen and opens the
refrigerator. He takes out a half-eaten McDonald's burger, a
few leftover fries, and a half-empty shake. He sits back at the
table. Opens them slowly, begins to eat. The phone rings.)*

GREGOR: *(Into the phone)* HELLO? THANK
YOU....Hello, Erna?...Lucie. It is Gregor. I wish to speak
to —. You don't know when she returns. What is she
seeing? Oh. Skreta's MACBETH. Tell her something for
me.... The critics did not like the production. No. They
said it was too European. You are right. She will be
very interested in that. Goodbye.

*(He hangs up. Sits for a moment. Then goes and turns the
television sound back on. And goes back to the table and eats
without watching.)*

TELEVISION: "— Accusing the United States of
torpedoing the possibility of agreement in Geneva, the
Soviet Union announced a further buildup of nuclear
weapons in Czechoslovakia and East Germany as well
as aboard submarines off the American coast. Whether
intentional or not, the effect was to link the fate of
Western Europe with that of the United States. Western
leaders reacted calmly. The President said he regretted
Moscow's attitude but professed confidence. 'I can't
believe it will be permanent,' he said."

END OF THE PLAY